a companion journal

Dr. Omar Suleiman

In association with

A *Du'a* Away: A Companion Journal

First published in England by
Kube Publishing Ltd
Markfield Conference Centre
Ratby Lane, Markfield
Leicestershire, LE67 9SY
United Kingdom

Tel: +44 (0) 1530 249230
Website: www.kubepublishing.com
Email: info@kubepublishing.com

 Cataloguing-in-Publication
Data is available from the British Library.

ISBN 978-1-84774-259-9 Paperback
Proofreading and editing: Yaqeen Institute
Layout and typesetting: Jannah Haque
Illustrations: Saarah Khan and Zhafri Kamarulzaman
Printed by: IMAK Ofset, Turkey.

Contents

Preface: Contentment is a *du'a* away

Du'a for contentment

اللَّهُمَّ قَنِّعْنِي بِمَا رَزَقْتَنِي، *Allahumma qanni'nee bimaa razzaqtanee*	**O Allah, make me content with the provision You have given me**
وَبَارِكْ لِي فِيهِ، *wa baarik lee feehi*	**and bless me in it**
وَاخْلُفْ عَلَيَّ كُلَّ غَائِبَةٍ لِي بِخَيْرٍ *wakhluf 'alayya kulla ghaa'ibatin lee bikhayr*	**and replace everything I have missed out on with that which is better for me.** [*Al-Adab al-Mufrad* 681]

Commentary

We often wonder whether it is appropriate to ask Allah for wealth and worldly possessions. There are many narrations that indicate that this is not only permissible, but that the Prophet ﷺ made *du'a* for some of his companions to receive a lot of wealth, like Anas ibn Malik ؓ. The Prophet ﷺ, however, knew who would benefit from a lot of wealth and only made that *du'a* for a select few. The more general prophetic *du'as* focus on contentment, having enough to suffice one's needs, and blessings in one's wealth.

The above narration is one such *du'a*. In this *du'a*, we ask Allah for three important bounties that are better than possessing a lot of wealth. The first is contentment with what we have, because contentment is the best type of wealth and calms the soul. The second is for *barakah* which means blessings, because a little bit that is blessed goes a long way. The third is to replace what is outside our destiny with that which is better for us, because Allah knows what is best for us, and He may deny us something we want because He knows that it is not best for us.

Reflections

Gems

Prophetic *du'as* revolutionise the way we view Allah, which revolutionises the way we view ourselves and the world around us.

The best *du'as* are not always about change in circumstance; often, they are about change in perspective.

Chapter 1

Change in *Qadar* is a *du'a* away

The most comprehensive *du'a*

Part 1
Everything that Allah knows

اللَّهُمَّ إِنِّي أَسْأَلُكَ مِنَ الْخَيْرِ كُلِّهِ عَاجِلِهِ
وَآجِلِهِ مَا عَلِمْتُ مِنْهُ وَمَا لَمْ أَعْلَمْ
وَأَعُوذُ بِكَ مِنَ الشَّرِّ كُلِّهِ عَاجِلِهِ وَآجِلِهِ
مَا عَلِمْتُ مِنْهُ وَمَا لَمْ أَعْلَمْ

Allahumma innee as'aluka min al-khayri kullihi 'aajilihi wa-aajilihi maa 'alimtu minhu wa-maa lam a'lam. Wa a'oodhu bika min ash-sharri kullihi 'aajilihi wa-aajilihi maa 'alimtu minhu wa-maa lam a'lam

O Allah, I ask You from all that is good, in this world and in the hereafter, of what I know and what I do not know. O Allah, I seek refuge with You from all evil, in this world and in the hereafter, of what I know and what I do not know.

Part 2
Everything the Prophet ﷺ asked for

اللَّهُمَّ إِنِّي أَسْأَلُكَ مِنْ خَيْرِ مَا سَأَلَكَ
عَبْدُكَ وَنَبِيُّكَ وَأَعُوذُ بِكَ مِنْ شَرِّ
مَا عَاذَ بِهِ عَبْدُكَ وَنَبِيُّكَ

Allahumma innee as'aluka min khayri maa sa'alaka 'abduka wa-nabeeyuka wa a'oodhu bika min sharri maa 'aadha bihi 'abduka wa-nabeeyuk

O Allah, I ask You for the good that Your slave and Prophet has asked You for, and I seek refuge with You from the evil from which Your slave and Prophet sought refuge.

Part 3
Everything that leads to the hereafter

اللَّهُمَّ إِنِّي أَسْأَلُكَ الْجَنَّةَ وَمَا قَرَّبَ إِلَيْهَا
مِنْ قَوْلٍ أَوْ عَمَلٍ وَأَعُوذُ بِكَ مِنَ النَّارِ
وَمَا قَرَّبَ إِلَيْهَا مِنْ قَوْلٍ أَوْ عَمَلٍ

Allahumma innee as'aluka al-jannata wa maa qarraba ilayha min qawlin aw 'amalin wa a'oodhu bika min an-naari wa maa qarraba ilayha min qawlin aw 'amalin

O Allah, I ask You for Paradise and for that which brings one closer to it, in word and deed. And I seek refuge in You from Hell and from that which brings one closer to it, in word and deed.

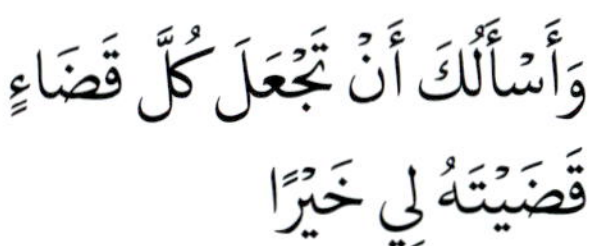

wa as'aluka an taj'ala kulla qadaa'in qadaytahu lee khayra

Part 4
Everything beneficial of Decree in this world

And I ask You to make every Decree that You decree concerning me good.
[*Sunan Ibn Majah* 3846]

Commentary

The Prophet ﷺ taught his wife A'ishah ﷺ what many scholars refer to as the most comprehensive *du'a*. This *du'a* covers every type of goodness, which can be broken down into four groups: what Allah knows is best for us, what the Prophet ﷺ asked for, everything that leads to Paradise, and anything good to be destined for us. The first part of this *du'a* covers everything that we want to ask Allah for, while deferring to His Perfect Knowledge as only Allah knows what is truly beneficial for us.

The second part of the *du'a* covers every narrated *du'a* because we are asking for everything the Prophet ﷺ asked for, and seeking protection from everything he sought protection from. The third part of the *du'a* is thorough regarding our afterlife. It is a *du'a* for Paradise and protection from Hellfire, specifically asking Allah for deeds and words that lead to Paradise, and for protection from deeds and words that lead to Hellfire, as it has been narrated that people's speech often subjects them to punishment in the hereafter. The final part of the *du'a* includes everything decreed for us, which is all good for us as long as we are patient with the trials and grateful for the blessings.

Reflections

Chapter 1

Change in *Qadar* is a *du'a* away

Du'a for protection from bad Decree

اللَّهُمَّ إِنِّي أَعُوذُ بِكَ مِنْ جَهْدِ الْبَلَاءِ، *Allahumma innee a'oodhu bika min jahd il-balaa'i*	**I seek refuge in Allah from severe calamity,**
وَدَرَكِ الشَّقَاءِ، *wa darak ish-shaqaa'i*	**being overtaken by misery, harmful destiny,**
وَسُوءِ الْقَضَاءِ، وَشَمَاتَةِ الأَعْدَاءِ *wa soo' il-qadaa'i wa shamaatat il-a'daa'i*	**and the gloating of enemies.** [*Sahih al-Bukhari* 6616]

Commentary

This *du'a* seeks protection from four broad categories of trials. The first is severe trials that are unbearable and make life difficult. The second is from being overwhelmed by trials, or when life gets so hard that one loses faith and hope. The third is harmful destiny, which includes when a trial takes us away from obeying Allah. The fourth is when our trials are so severe that they cause our enemies to gloat and find pleasure in our pain. We are taught in this supplication to seek Allah's protection from all of these.

Reflections

Du'a for contentment with Decree

اللَّهُمَّ إِنِّي أَسْأَلُكَ الرِّضَا بَعْدَ الْقَضَاءِ

Allahumma innee as'aluka ar-ridaa ba'd al-qadaa

O Allah, I ask you for contentment after the Decree.

[*Sunan an-Nasa'i* 1305]

Commentary

Life's journey is filled with challenges that test our strength and determination. When we encounter difficulties, it's common to feel overwhelmed. Yet, embracing the belief that Allah knows what's best for us can bring a sense of inner peace that transcends worldly joys. This is the essence of contentment. While we cannot control every aspect of our lives, being pleased with Allah's Decree enables us to navigate the ups and downs of life with tranquility.

Gems

Good Decree doesn't necessarily mean *easy* Decree. It could mean a hardship that brings you closer to Allah.

Being pleased with Allah and His Decree is the paradise of this earth, and the wisest *du'as* include seeking contentment.

Reflections

Chapter 2

Your decision is a *du'a* away

Du'a of Istikharah

اللَّهُمَّ إِنِّي أَسْتَخِيرُكَ بِعِلْمِكَ وَأَسْتَقْدِرُكَ
بِقُدْرَتِكَ، وَأَسْأَلُكَ مِنْ فَضْلِكَ الْعَظِيمِ،
فَإِنَّكَ تَقْدِرُ وَلَا أَقْدِرُ وَتَعْلَمُ وَلَا أَعْلَمُ
وَأَنْتَ عَلَّامُ الْغُيُوبِ

Allahumma innee astakheeruka bi 'ilmika wa astaqdiruka bi qudratika wa as'aluka min fadlika al-'adheem fa innaka taqdiru wa la aqdiru wa ta'lamu wa la a'lamu wa anta 'allaam ul-ghuyoob

O Allah, I seek Your guidance (in making a choice) by virtue of Your knowledge, and I seek ability by virtue of Your power, and I ask You of Your great bounty. You have power, and I do not. You know, and I know not, and You are the Knower of the Unseen.

اللَّهُمَّ إِنْ كُنْتَ تَعْلَمُ أَنَّ هَذَا الْأَمْرَ
خَيْرٌ لِي فِي دِينِي وَمَعَاشِي وَعَاقِبَةِ أَمْرِي
فَاقْدُرْهُ لِي وَيَسِّرْهُ لِي ثُمَّ بَارِكْ لِي فِيهِ

Allahumma in kunta ta'lamu anna haadha al-amra khayrun lee fee deenee wa ma'aashee wa 'aaqibati amree faqdurhu lee wa yassirhu lee thumma baarik lee feehi

O Allah, if You know that this matter [*mention the thing to be decided*] is good for me in my religion, my livelihood, my worldly affairs, and in the hereafter then decree it for me, make it easy for me, and bless it for me.

وَإِنْ كُنْتَ تَعْلَمُ أَنَّ هَذَا الْأَمْرَ شَرٌّ لِي
فِي دِينِي وَمَعَاشِي وَعَاقِبَةِ أَمْرِي فَاصْرِفْهُ
عَنِّي وَاصْرِفْنِي عَنْهُ، وَاقْدُرْ لِيَ الْخَيْرَ
حَيْثُ كَانَ ثُمَّ أَرْضِنِي بِهِ

wa in kunta ta'lamu anna haadha al-amara sharrun lee fee deenee wa ma'aashee wa 'aaqibati amree fasrifhu 'annee wasrifnee 'anhu waqdur lil-khayra haythu kaana thumma ardinee bih

And if You know that this matter is bad for me in my religion, my livelihood, my worldly affairs, and in the hereafter then turn it away from me and turn me away from it, and decree for me the good wherever it may be and make me content with it.

[*Sahih al-Bukhari* 6382]

Commentary

The *du'a* of *Istikharah* is one of the most important *du'as* to memorise and utilise often. A common misconception is that this *du'a* is only for key decisions like marriage or starting a business. The early generations would seek Allah's guidance for many matters, including things that we may consider light. The key is to avoid rushing into decisions and to consult Allah at every stage of our lives.

There are some misconceptions about *Istikharah* that need to be clarified. It is not a magic *du'a* that gives you what you want. It is also not necessarily linked to dreams. It is simply a means of consulting Allah, trusting Him, and handing over your affair to Him. We should not expect any signs or dreams after *Istikharah*. It is a *du'a* for guidance.

The proper method is to do our research, consult experts and those who care about our well-being, and then ask Allah to guide us to make the right decision. *Istikharah* is performed by making the intention, praying two optional *rak'ah*, and then making this *du'a* after the *salah*. It can even be prayed daily, for multiple reasons especially when making decisions with unclear consequences.

Gems

Trusting in Allah doesn't just mean trusting in His Power. It also means trusting in His Wisdom.

Life without praying *Salat al-Istikharah* is like *salah* without reciting Qur'an.

Reflections

Chapter 3

Allah is a *du'a* away

Don't say "insha'Allah" in *du'a*

عَنْ أَنَسٍ ﵁ قَالَ قَالَ رَسُولُ اللَّهِ ﷺ
إِذَا دَعَا أَحَدُكُمْ فَلْيَعْزِمْ فِي الدُّعَاءِ
وَلاَ يَقُلِ اللَّهُمَّ إِنْ شِئْتَ فَأَعْطِنِي
فَإِنَّ اللَّهَ لاَ مُسْتَكْرِهَ لَه

It is reported by Anas ﵁ that the Messenger of Allah ﷺ said, "When one of you calls upon Allah, let him be determined in the supplication and not say, 'O Allah, give me *if You will*,' for there is no one to coerce Allah."
[*Sahih al-Bukhari* 6338; *Sahih Muslim* 2678]

Commentary

A common mistake is to say "insha'Allah" (if Allah wills) at the end of a *du'a*. The Prophet ﷺ taught us to avoid such phrasing as it lessens the impact and potency of the *du'a*. We must ask Allah with full certainty, especially when we know what we are asking for is good for us. Saying insha'Allah in a *du'a* is like saying "O Allah, give it to me if you want to" or "Forgive me if you want to." When translated, it becomes clearer that this wording is inappropriate, suggesting a lack of genuine need for the thing you are requesting.

Furthermore, nobody can force Allah to do anything; He only does what He wills. Therefore, the phrase "if You will" is unnecessary when addressing Allah because He is not subject to coercion or compulsion. We must ask Allah with full conviction and hope that He will grant our requests. It is important to remember that while saying insha'Allah is appropriate when talking about the future, it is generally considered bad etiquette when making *du'a*. Have firm faith that the Most Merciful will answer your *du'a*, and ask with confidence and certainty.

Reflections

Gems

Call out to Allah desperately, but confidently. Allah does not tire of answering you until you tire of asking Him.

Allah answered the *du'a* of the worst creation, Iblis, when he asked for respite until Judgement Day. Don't let your shortcomings keep you from asking Allah.

Chapter 4

Companionship is a *du'a* away

Du'a for companionship

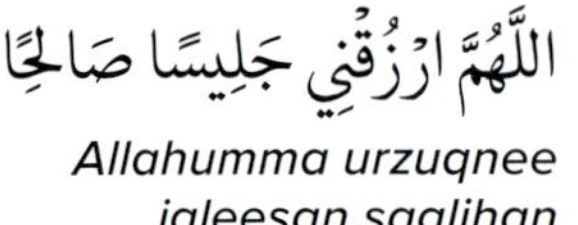

Allahumma urzuqnee jaleesan saalihan

O Allah, grant me righteous company.
[*Jami' at-Tirmidhi* 413]

Commentary

The people in our lives are also a part of our sustenance (*rizq*). Allah destined for us to meet people in this world that bring value and goodness to our lives. Our *du'as* can also lead us to meet people who become dear to us and change our lives. It is narrated that one of the early Muslims made this *du'a* before going to the masjid where he met Abu ad-Darda ﷺ, one of the great companions. This was the beginning of a beautiful friendship, a response to his *du'a*.

Reflections

Du'a for *rizq*

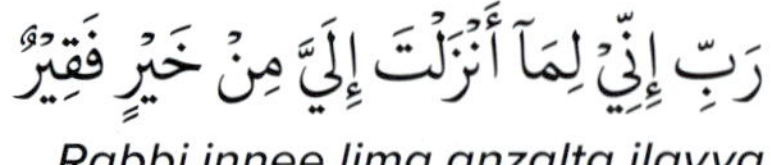

Rabbi innee lima anzalta ilayya min khayrin faqeer

My Lord! I am truly in need of whatever provision You may have in store for me.

[Qur'an, 28:24]

Commentary

Most of the *du'as* for companionship are not detailed. We ask Allah for what is best for us, trusting that He knows what is best for us. Prophet Musa ﷺ made this *du'a* during one of the most difficult moments of his life. He had fled Egypt to escape the Pharaoh and was alone in a new land without any shelter or income. He asked Allah for any goodness. In response to his *du'a*, Allah gave him a new home, a wife, a family, and a job. This is one of the best *du'as* to make to Allah when seeking a spouse or anything that you need in life. The *du'a* is generic because only Allah knows what is ultimately good for us.

Reflections

Du'a of the divorced and widowed

إِنَّا لِلَّهِ وَإِنَّا إِلَيْهِ رَاجِعُونَ

Inna lillahi wa inna ilayhi raji'oon

Verily, to Allah we belong, and to Him we will return.
[Qur'an, 2:156]

اللَّهُمَّ أَجُرْنِي فِي مُصِيبَتِي،
وأَخْلِفْ لِي خَيْرًا مِنْهَا

Allahumma ajurnee fee museebati wa akhlif lee khayran minha

O Allah, reward me for my affliction and give me something better than it.
[*Sahih Muslim* 918]

Commentary

This is the famous *du'a* Umm Salama ﵂ made when her beloved husband Abu Salama ﵁ passed away. She could not imagine any man being better than Abu Salama ﵁, but she made this *du'a* frequently. Umm Salama ﵂ would eventually marry the Prophet ﷺ, which is the best possible answer to her beautiful *du'a*.

Reflections

The comprehensive *du'a* for marriage and family

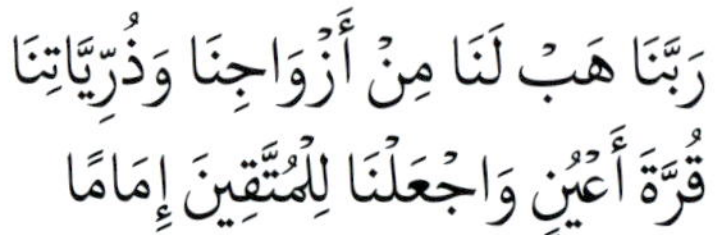

Rabbana hab lana min azwaajinaa wa dhurriyaatinaa qurrata a'yunin waj'alnaa lil-muttaqeena imaama

Our Lord, grant us delight in our spouses and our children, and make us a good example for the righteous.
[Qur'an, 25:74]

Commentary

This is the most comprehensive *du'a* for a spouse, mentioned in the Qur'an as a *du'a* that the righteous make often. This *du'a* teaches us to become righteous people, so that we attract a righteous spouse and are able to raise righteous children. We should make *du'a* at every stage of life, both before and during marriage. Before marriage, it is a *du'a* for a righteous spouse. During marriage, it is a *du'a* for oneself and one's spouse to grow in righteousness, as well as a *du'a* for one's children or future children's righteousness too.

Reflections

Gems

Sometimes, simply presenting your situation to Allah is even more powerful than directly asking Allah.

You don't have to know *exactly* what to ask of Allah. You just need to know that delegating your affairs to the Most Wise will garner the best response.

Chapter 5

Long life is a *du'a* away

Du'a for a fulfilling life

اللَّهُمَّ إِنِّي أَسْأَلُكَ فِعْلَ الْخَيْرَاتِ وَتَرْكَ الْمُنْكَرَاتِ وَحُبَّ الْمَسَاكِينِ

Allahumma innee as'aluka fi'l al-khayraat wa tark al-munkaraat wa hubb al-masaakeen

O Allah! Indeed I ask You for righteous deeds, and avoiding evil deeds, and loving the poor.

وَإِذَا أَرَدْتَ فِي النَّاسِ فِتْنَةً فَاقْبِضْنِي إِلَيْكَ غَيْرَ مَفْتُونٍ

wa idha aradta fi an-naasi fitnatan faqbidnee ilayka ghayra maftoon

And if you have willed a trial for people, then take me to You, without being put to trial.

[*Jami' at-Tirmidhi* 3233]

Commentary

The life and death of a believer is for Allah. We live for Allah, and work towards a good ending and eternal Paradise. One of the signs of the Day of Judgement is that a person walks by a grave and wishes he was in it, not out of a desire to meet Allah but to escape life. Others cling to this world due to their love for it, forgetting to prepare for the afterlife. The Prophet ﷺ taught us many *du'as* that focus on the afterlife and deeds that lead to a good ending and eternal bliss.

In this *du'a*, we are taught the importance of righteous deeds and avoiding sin. Righteous deeds lead to Paradise, while sins can lead to divine punishment. The *du'a* includes love of the poor because many of the greatest deeds involve taking care of the poor. Interestingly, the last part of the *du'a* is a request for Allah to take one's life if a significant trial is about to befall one's people. This refers to trials that threaten one's faith because it is better to die upon righteousness than to lose faith through a difficult trial. Trials that bring us closer to Allah, however, are actually beneficial for us.

Du'a for the best time of death

اللَّهُمَّ أَحْيِنِي مَا كَانَتِ الْحَيَاةُ خَيْرًا لِي
وَتَوَفَّنِي إِذَا كَانَتِ الْوَفَاةُ خَيْرًا لِي

Allahumma ahyinee maa kaanat il-hayaatu khayran lee wa tawaffanee idha kaanat il-wafaatu khayran lee

O Allah, keep me alive as long as You know that life is better for me, and cause me to die when death is better for me.

[*Sahih al-Bukhari* 5671]

Commentary

Allah alone knows best whether a long life or a short life is good for us. This *du'a* teaches us to put our trust in Allah's Perfect Knowledge. We wish to live as long as life is pleasing to Allah and a means of drawing closer to Him. However, if life becomes a trial that takes us away from Allah, we pray that Allah takes us to Him before such a trial can affect us. The Prophet ﷺ taught us to make this *du'a* when life gets hard instead of wishing for death. This way we leave the matter to Allah's Perfect Knowledge and Decree.

Gems

Believers do not seek death to avoid hardships. They see life as a chance to please Allah, and a longer life means more opportunities to perform good deeds.

Believers love and are grateful to the One Who determines the perfect moment for their arrival on Earth and their departure from it.

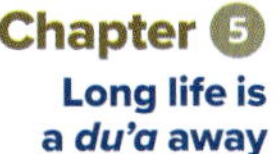

Reflections

Chapter 6

Protection is a *du'a* away

Du’a for protection from every harm

x3 in the morning
x3 in the evening

بِسْمِ اللهِ

Bismillahi

In the Name of Allah,

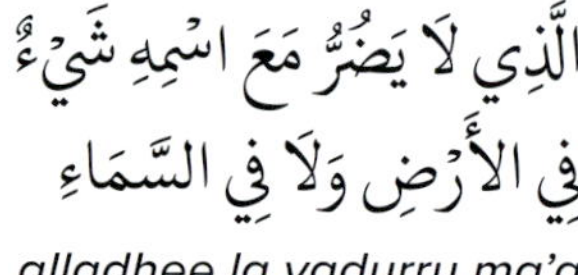

alladhee la yadurru ma’a ismihi shay’un fee al-ardi wa la fee as-samaa’i

with Whose Name nothing is harmed on the earth nor in heaven,

وَهُوَ السَّمِيعُ العَلِيمُ

wa huwa as-samee’u al-’aleem

and He is the All-Hearing, the All-Knowing.

[*Jami’ at-Tirmidhi* 3388]

Commentary

The first two *du’as* in this chapter are from the recommended morning and evening *du’as*. It is recommended to recite these *du’as* every morning after Fajr and every evening after Asr or Maghrib to ward off potential harms and trials from our future that only Allah knows. With this *du’a*, we preemptively seek Allah’s protection from any harm in our future that we cannot see and know about.

If we make this *du’a* regularly but still face harm, we should accept it as Allah’s Decree, which is ultimately good for us. Allah protects us as He sees fit, and whatever happens is ultimately good, even if we don't understand why. Nonetheless, this *du’a* is effective in keeping us safe from harm, often protecting us without us even realising.

Reflections

Du'a for good health and protection from trials

x3 in the morning
x3 in the evening

اللَّهُمَّ عَافِنِي فِي بَدَنِي، اللَّهُمَّ عَافِنِي فِي سَمْعِي، اللَّهُمَّ عَافِنِي فِي بَصَرِي، لَا إِلَهَ إِلَّا أَنْتَ

Allahumma 'aafinee fee badanee, Allahumma 'aafinee fee sam'ee, Allahumma 'aafinee fee basaree, la ilaha illa anta

O Allah, make me healthy in my body. O Allah, make me healthy in my hearing. O Allah, make me healthy in my sight. There is no god but You.

اللَّهُمَّ إِنِّي أَعُوذُ بِكَ مِنَ الْكُفْرِ وَالْفَقْرِ، اللَّهُمَّ إِنِّي أَعُوذُ بِكَ مِنْ عَذَابِ الْقَبْرِ، لَا إِلَهَ إِلَّا أَنْتَ

Allahumma innee a'oodhu bika min al-kufri wal-faqri, Allahumma innee a'oodhu bika min 'adhaab il-qabri la ilaha illa anta

O Allah, I seek refuge with You from disbelief and poverty. O Allah, I seek refuge with You from the punishment of the grave. There is no god but You.

[*Sunan Abi Dawud* 5090]

Commentary

This is a comprehensive *du'a* that should be made every morning and evening, three times each. The first half of the *du'a* focuses on worldly trials affecting our health. Over time, many people lose their eyesight and hearing, and their health deteriorates. While this *du'a* is a preventative measure against these trials, we still need to live a healthy life and do what is needed to preserve these blessings. The second half of the *du'a* focusses on some of the most difficult trials in our religion: losing faith and poverty. The *du'a* ends with protection from the punishment of the grave.

Reflections

Du'a for relief from hardship

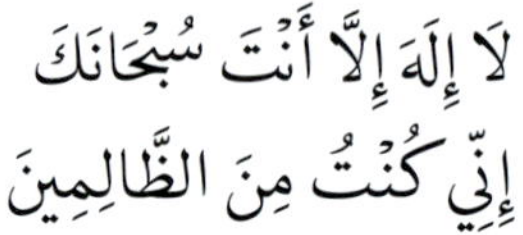

La ilaha illa anta subhaanaka innee kuntu min adh-dhalimeen

There is no god but You, glorified are You, indeed I am one of the wrongdoers.
[Qur'an, 21:87]

Commentary

This is the *du'a* of Prophet Yunus ﷺ when he was in the belly of the whale. It is recommended to make this *du'a* when a trial occurs and you do not know how to get out of it. Just like Allah helped Prophet Yunus ﷺ escape the belly of the whale, He can help us out of any trial. This *du'a* is a humble acknowledgement of our own sins and faults, while recognizing the perfection of Allah. This dual recognition unlocks divine assistance in unimaginable ways.

Gems

Oftentimes, you may trust Allah to relieve you of hardships that you *know* are in your life. But your preventative *du'as* work in your favour every day, blocking hardships you didn't even know were coming your way.

When you acknowledge your vulnerability to Allah, especially in a moment of hardship, Allah will not just remove that hardship—He'll give you things that you didn't even know you needed.

Reflections

Chapter 7

Relief is a *du'a* away

Du'a to replace anxiety with peace

اللَّهُمَّ إِنِّي عَبْدُكَ ابْنُ عَبْدِكَ ابْنُ أَمَتِكَ

Allahumma innee 'abduka ibnu 'abdika ibnu amatika

O Allah, I am Your slave, and the son of Your male slave, and the son of Your female slave.

نَاصِيَتِي بِيَدِكَ مَاضٍ فِيَّ حُكْمُكَ عَدْلٌ فِيَّ قَضَاؤُكَ

naasiyatee biyadika maadin fiyya hukmuka 'adlun fiyya qadaa'uka

My forehead is in Your Hand [i.e., You have control over me]. Your Judgement upon me is assured, and Your Decree concerning me is just.

أَسْأَلُكَ بِكُلِّ اسْمٍ هُوَ لَكَ سَمَّيْتَ بِهِ نَفْسَكَ أَوْ أَنْزَلْتَهُ فِي كِتَابِكَ أَوْ عَلَّمْتَهُ أَحَدًا مِنْ خَلْقِكَ أَوِ اسْتَأْثَرْتَ بِهِ فِي عِلْمِ الغَيْبِ عِنْدَكَ

as'aluka bi kulli ismin huwa laka sammayta bihi nafsaka aw anzaltahu fee kitaabika aw 'ullamtahu ahadan min khalqika aw ista'tharta bihi fee 'ilm al-ghaybi 'indaka

I ask You by every Name with which You have named Yourself, whether you revealed in Your Scripture, taught any one of Your creation, or kept unto Yourself in the knowledge of the Unseen that is with You,

أَنْ تَجْعَلَ القُرْآنَ رَبِيعَ قَلْبِي وَنُورَ صَدْرِي وَجَلَاءَ حُزْنِي وذَهَابَ هَمِّي

an taj'ala al-Qur'ana rabee'a qalbee wa noora sadree wa jalaa'a huznee wa dhahaaba hammee

to make the Qur'an the spring of my heart, and the light of my chest, the lifting of my sadness, and the departure of my anxiety.

[*Musnad Ahmad* 1:391]

Commentary

The Prophet ﷺ said that whoever experiences anxiety should make this *du'a* and Allah will replace his anxiety with inner peace and contentment. This *du'a* starts with a reminder that we are the slaves of Allah, as are our parents, so we submit to Allah and accept that He is our Lord, and only Allah can help us. This is followed by an admission that Allah knows and decrees what is best for us. The *du'a* includes a call to Allah by all of His Perfect Names, including names that we do not know.

Finally, the *du'a* ends with asking Allah to make the Qur'an our source of relief. The Qur'an is the word of Allah and a cure for every spiritual illness. We are directed in this part of the *du'a* to turn to the Qur'an for guidance and relief. To be effective, we must recite the Qur'an and engage with it. The message of the Qur'an puts worldly trials into perspective and grants us relief and calmness even during the toughest of trials.

Reflections

Du'a for relief from worries and debt

اللَّهُمَّ إِنِّي أَعُوذُ بِكَ مِنَ الْهَمِّ وَالْحَزَنِ،

Allahumma innee a'oodhu bika min al-hammi wal-hazani

O Allah! I seek refuge in You from worry and grief,

وَأَعُوذُ بِكَ مِنَ الْعَجْزِ وَالْكَسَلِ،

wa a'oodhu bika min al-'ajzi wal-kasali

and I seek refuge in You from incapacity and laziness,

وَأَعُوذُ بِكَ مِنَ الْجُبْنِ وَالْبُخْلِ،

wa a'oodhu bika min al-jubni wal-bukhli

and I seek refuge in You from cowardice and miserliness,

وَأَعُوذُ بِكَ مِنْ غَلَبَةِ الدَّيْنِ، وَقَهْرِ الرِّجَالِ

wa a'oodhu bika min ghalabat id-dayni wa qahr ir-rijaal

and I seek refuge in You from the burden of debt and oppression of men.

[*Sahih al-Bukhari* 6369]

Commentary

The Prophet ﷺ taught this *du'a* to a Companion who was overwhelmed with worry and debt. This *du'a* covers protection from eight categories of worldly trials. The first four are emotional trials: anxiety, grief, inability and laziness. The next two are negative characteristics: cowardice and miserliness. The last two trials are from other people, which is debt and tyranny. We seek Allah's protection daily from all these trials.

Reflections

Du'a to remove anger

اللَّهُمَّ رَبَّ مُحَمَّدٍ اغْفِرْ لِي ذَنْبِي، وَأَذْهِبْ غَيْظَ قَلْبِي، وَأَعِذْنِي مِنْ مُضِلَّاتِ الْفِتَنِ

Allahumma rabba Muhammadin ighfir lee dhanbee wa adhhib ghaydha qalbee wa a'idhnee min mudillaat il-fitan

O Allah, Lord of Muhammad! Forgive my sins, remove the anger of my heart, and protect me from misleading trials.

[*Musnad Ahmad* 26576]

Commentary

The Prophet ﷺ taught this *du'a* to his wife A'ishah ؓ as a means of protection from being overwhelmed by one's emotions, specifically anger. Anger is a natural human emotion that must be regulated. If we allow it to overwhelm us and control us, it can lead to a lot of regrets. So we are encouraged to regularly seek Allah's protection from anger and the trials it can lead to.

Gems

One of the most effective ways to have your *du'a* answered is to call upon Allah by His Names. Imagine how comprehensively effective it is to include "I ask You by every Name" in a *du'a*!

Even when Allah has removed your hardship, you may still feel its emotional impact for a long time. But the Prophet's ﷺ comprehensive *du'as* teach us that even how we feel can be changed.

Reflections

Chapter 8

Changing your heart is a *du'a* away

Du'a to protect the heart

رَبَّنَا لَا تُزِغْ قُلُوبَنَا بَعْدَ إِذْ هَدَيْتَنَا وَهَبْ لَنَا مِن لَّدُنكَ رَحْمَةً إِنَّكَ أَنتَ ٱلْوَهَّابُ

Rabbana la tuzigh quloobanaa ba'da idh hadaytanaa wa hab lana min ludnka rahmatan innaka anta al-wahhaab

Our Lord! Do not let our hearts deviate after You have guided us, and grant us from Yourself mercy. Indeed You, You are the Bestower.

[Qur'an, 3:8]

Commentary

The heart is literally the center of our being and must be safeguarded from evil influences. If we allow the whisperings of Satan or the whims of the ego to overcome it, it could very well ruin our entire being. This *du'a* protects our hearts from misguidance. Our hearts are in Allah's Hands, and the most important parl of us. If it strays, everything else strays with it. So we seek Allah's protection regularly from our hearts deviating.

We should not take guidance for granted or feel entitled to it. The state of the heart is always changing, so we should constantly seek steadfastness and guidance.

Reflections

Du'a to remove grudges

رَبَّنَا اغْفِرْ لَنَا وَلِإِخْوَانِنَا الَّذِينَ سَبَقُونَا بِالإِيمَانِ وَلَا تَجْعَلْ فِي قُلُوبِنَا غِلًّا لِّلَّذِينَ آمَنُوا رَبَّنَا إِنَّكَ رَؤُوفٌ رَّحِيمٌ

Rabbana ighfir lana wa li-ikhwaaninaa alladheena sabaqoona bil-eemaani wa la taj'al fee quloobinaa ghillan lilladheena aamanoo rabbana innaka ra'oofun raheem

Our Lord, forgive us and our brethren who preceded us in faith, and leave no malice in our hearts towards those who believe. Our Lord, You are Clement and Merciful.

[Qur'an, 59:10]

Commentary

This *du'a* seeks protection from hatred or envy towards fellow Muslims. It is part of life that some people may have gifts and privileges that others do not. We should always look at these gifts as part of Allah's Destiny, and recognise that Allah knows best how to distribute His blessings. Unity between believers is necessary, and breaking ties with a Muslim is a major sin. To avoid this, we should regularly seek Allah's protection from any negative emotions entering our hearts and affecting our relationship with others.

Reflections

The most frequent *du'a* of the Prophet ﷺ

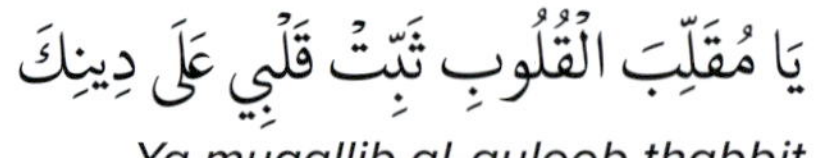

Ya muqallib al-quloob thabbit qalbee 'ala deenik

O Turner of hearts, make my heart firm on Your path.
[*Jami' at-Tirmidhi* 3522]

Commentary

This is the most frequent *du'a* that the Prophet ﷺ used to make. He taught us to make this *du'a* regularly because the state of the heart is constantly changing, and only Allah has control over our hearts. We must seek His divine aid in keeping our hearts steadfast in obeying Him and staying guided.

The Prophet ﷺ said, "The parable of the heart is that of a feather blown about by the wind of the desert." [*Sunan Ibn Majah* 88]

Reflections

Chapter 8

Changing your heart is *du'a* away

Du'a for a heart obedient to Allah

اللَّهُمَّ مُصَرِّفَ الْقُلُوبِ
صَرِّفْ قُلُوبَنَا عَلَى طَاعَتِكَ

Allahumma musarrif al-quloob sarrif quloobanaa 'ala taa'atik

O Allah, Turner of hearts, turn our hearts towards your obedience.
[*Sahih Muslim* 2655]

Commentary

This is a variation of the above *du'a*. The first version is a *du'a* for steadfastness on the straight path. The second variation is a *du'a* for guidance to deeds that keep us on the straight path. We must make both *du'as* regularly while doing righteous deeds. Righteous deeds are the vehicle through which these *du'as* are answered.

The Prophet ﷺ said, "Verily, in the body is a piece of flesh which, if sound, the entire body is sound, but if corrupt, the entire body is corrupt. Truly, it is the heart." [*Sahih al-Bukhari* 52]

Reflections

Gems

The more that your heart is occupied by Allah, the more present it will be in *du'a*, and the more you'll find yourself guided to what's pleasing to Him.

The more that you allow your heart to become full of your desires, distractions, or grudges, the less capacity your heart will have for Allah.

A pure heart is one that is pious, without sin, injustice, malice, or envy. The Prophet's ﷺ heart was the purest, yet his most frequent *du'a* was to keep it that way.

One of the best ways to keep your heart firm upon guidance is to be someone who is concerned about the guidance of others, frequently making *du'a* for them.

Chapter 9

Salvation on Arafah is a *du'a* away

Du'a to be freed from the Fire

اللَّهُمَّ أَعْتِقْ رَقَبَتِي مِنَ النَّارِ،

Allahumma a'tiq raqabatee min an-naari

O Allah, free my neck from the Fire,

وَأَوْسِعْ لِي مِنَ الرِّزْقِ الْحَلَالِ،

wa-awsi' lee min ar-rizq il-halaal

bestow on me halal sustenance,

وَاصْرِفْ عَنِّي فَسَقَةَ الْجِنِّ وَالْإِنْسِ

wasrif 'annee fasaqat al-jinni wal-ins

and avert from me corrupt jinn and men.

[*Ibn Abi Dunya*]

Commentary

The day of Arafah is a day in which *du'as* are answered and people are forgiven for their sins. The Prophet ﷺ said, "There is no day in which Allah sets free more souls from the fire of Hell than on the day of Arafah. He draws near and then He boasts of them to the angels, saying: What do these servants want?" [*Sahih Muslim* 1348] It is recommended to recite this *du'a*, narrated by Ali ibn Abi Talib ؓ, on the day of Arafah. This is for all believers wherever they are in the world, and it is not limited to the people at the plains of Arafat.

This *du'a* has three parts. The first is a prayer for freedom from the fire which includes forgiveness for our sins, as well as guidance to righteous deeds. The second part is a *du'a* for halal sustenance, and the third is asking for protection from all worldly evil. This comprehensive *du'a* covers everything we need in this world and the next.

Reflections

The best *du'a* on the day of Arafah

لَا إِلَٰهَ إِلَّا اللَّهُ وَحْدَهُ لَا شَرِيكَ لَهُ *La ilaha illa Allahu wahdahu la shareeka lahu*	**There is no true deity but God alone who has no partner;**
لَهُ الْمُلْكُ وَلَهُ الْحَمْدُ *lahul-mulku wa lahul-hamdu*	**to Him belongs the dominion, to Him praise is due,**
وَهُوَ عَلَىٰ كُلِّ شَيْءٍ قَدِيرٌ *wa huwa 'ala kulli shay'in qadeer*	**and He is able to do all things.** [*Sunan at-Tirmidhi* 3585]

Commentary

The Prophet ﷺ said, "The best supplication is that on the day of Arafah, and the best thing which I and the prophets before me have said is, 'There is no true deity but God alone who has no partner; to Him belongs the dominion, to Him praise is due, and He is able to do all things.'" [*Sunan al-Tirmidhi* 3585]

This is a day in which all *du'as* are answered. Every Muslim anywhere in the world should make time on this day to call on Allah. The worst state to be in on this day is to think that Allah will not answer your *du'as*, so you do not make *du'a* and deprive yourself of these blessings. Always maintain good assumptions about Allah, and be confident that He will answer your *du'as* regardless of your shortcomings and weaknesses.

Reflections

Gems

There should be no greater desire on the day of Arafah than to be amongst those freed from the Fire.

The best *du'as* combine presenting your own weakness to Allah with acknowledgment of His greatness.

Chapter 10

The best of everything is a *du'a* away

Du'a that covers all needs

اللَّهُمَّ إِنِّي أَسْأَلُكَ الْعَافِيَةَ فِي الدُّنْيَا وَالآخِرَةِ

Allahumma innee as'aluka al-'afiyah fid-dunyaa wal-aakhirah

O Allah, I ask you for *'afiyah* in this life and the next.
[*Sunan Ibn Majah* 3871]

Commentary

The Prophet's ﷺ uncle Abbas ؓ asked him which *du'a* to make through which all his needs would be taken care of. The Prophet ﷺ advised him to make *du'a* for *'afiyah* in this world and the next. *'Afiyah*, which means to be free of illnesses and afflictions, is much more than physical health. It includes spiritual, emotional, and social dimensions of well-being. However, if we are tested with hardships, we should remain patient and steadfast and continue to ask Allah for *'afiyah.*

Reflections

Chapter 10

The best of everything is a *du'a* away

Du'a for the best of both worlds

اللَّهُمَّ اغْفِرْ لَنَا، وَارْحَمْنَا،
Allahumma ighfir lana warhamnaa

O Allah, forgive us, have mercy on us,

وَآتِنَا فِي الدُّنْيَا حَسَنَةً، وَفِي الْآخِرَةِ حَسَنَةً،
wa 'aatinaa fid-dunyaa hasanatan wa fil-aakhirati hasanatan

and grant us the best of this life, and the best of the afterlife,

وَقِنَا عَذَابَ النَّارِ
wa qinaa 'adhaab an-naar

and protect us from the fire.
[*Al-Adab al-Mufrad* 633]

Commentary

The best *du'as* include this world and the next. This *du'a* is similar to the famous *du'a* from the Qur'an and covers the same three categories: goodness in this world, goodness in the hereafter (i.e., Paradise), and protection from Hellfire. This short *du'a* holistically covers everything we need in this world and the next.

Two thirds of this *du'a* focusses on the afterlife, and one third on this world. This teaches us to prioritise the afterlife in our actions and *du'a* and work towards Paradise. At the same time, we should not neglect the permissible enjoyment of this world in a manner that does not harm our faith.

Reflections

A comprehensive *du'a* to recite in salah

اللَّهُمَّ اغْفِرْ لِي، وَارْحَمْنِي، *Allahumma ighfir lee warhamnee*	**O Allah, forgive me, show mercy to me,**
وَاهْدِنِي، وَارْزُقْنِي *wahdinee warzuqnee*	**guide me, and provide for me.** [*Sahih Muslim* 2697]

Commentary

This short comprehensive *du'a* covers the four blessings we all need the most: Allah's forgiveness, His Mercy, guidance to that which is pleasing to Allah, and provisions in this world. Like the above *du'a*, most of this *du'a* focusses on the afterlife. Forgiveness protects us from Hellfire, while guidance leads to Paradise. The final portion of this *du'a* focusses on this world by asking for good sustenance that is sufficient and blessed, once again showing us the importance of prioritising the afterlife without neglecting our portion of this world.

Gems

It's not about the increase of words. It's about knowing the One you're calling upon.

These short *du'as* can change your entire world and hereafter, so long as you are sincere.

Reflections

Du'as recap

Preface: Contentment is a *du'a* away

Du'a for contentment

اللَّهُمَّ قَنِّعْنِي بِمَا رَزَقْتَنِي، وَبَارِكْ لِي فِيهِ، وَاخْلُفْ عَلَيَّ كُلَّ غَائِبَةٍ لِي بِخَيْرٍ

Allahumma qanni'nee bimaa razzaqtanee baarik lee feehi wakhluf 'alayya kulla ghaa'ibatin lee bikhayr

O Allah, make me content with the provision You have given me and bless me in it and replace everything I have missed out on with that which is better for me.

[*Al-Adab al-Mufrad* 681]

Chapter 1

Change in *Qadar* is a *du'a* away

The most comprehensive *du'a*

اللَّهُمَّ إِنِّي أَسْأَلُكَ مِنَ الْخَيْرِ كُلِّهِ عَاجِلِهِ وَآجِلِهِ مَا عَلِمْتُ مِنْهُ وَمَا لَمْ أَعْلَمْ وَأَعُوذُ بِكَ مِنَ الشَّرِّ كُلِّهِ عَاجِلِهِ وَآجِلِهِ مَا عَلِمْتُ مِنْهُ وَمَا لَمْ أَعْلَمْ اللَّهُمَّ إِنِّي أَسْأَلُكَ مِنْ خَيْرِ مَا سَأَلَكَ عَبْدُكَ وَنَبِيُّكَ وَأَعُوذُ بِكَ مِنْ شَرِّ مَا عَاذَ بِهِ عَبْدُكَ وَنَبِيُّكَ اللَّهُمَّ إِنِّي أَسْأَلُكَ الْجَنَّةَ وَمَا قَرَّبَ إِلَيْهَا مِنْ قَوْلٍ أَوْ عَمَلٍ وَأَعُوذُ بِكَ مِنَ النَّارِ وَمَا قَرَّبَ إِلَيْهَا مِنْ قَوْلٍ أَوْ عَمَلٍ وَأَسْأَلُكَ أَنْ تَجْعَلَ كُلَّ قَضَاءٍ قَضَيْتَهُ لِي خَيْرًا

Allahumma innee as'aluka min al-khayri kullihi 'aajilihi wa-aajilihi maa 'alimtu minhu wa-maa lam a'lam. Wa a'oodhu bika min ash-sharri kullihi 'aajilihi wa-aajilihi maa 'alimtu minhu wa-maa lam a'lam. Allahumma innee as'aluka min khayri maa sa'alaka 'abduka wa-nabeeyuka wa a'oodhu bika min sharri maa 'aadha bihi 'abduka wa-nabeeyuk. Allahumma innee as'aluka al-jannata wa maa qarraba ilayha min qawlin aw 'amalin wa a'oodhu bika min an-naari wa maa qarraba ilayha min qawlin aw 'amalin wa as'aluka an taj'ala kulla qadaa'in qadaytahu lee khayra

O Allah, I ask You from all that is good, in this world and in the hereafter, of what I know and what I do not know. O Allah, I seek refuge with You from all evil, in this world and in the hereafter, of what I know and what I do not know. O Allah, I ask You for the good that Your slave and Prophet has asked You for, and I seek refuge with You from the evil from which Your slave and Prophet sought refuge. O Allah, I ask You for Paradise and for that which brings one closer to it, in word and deed. And I seek refuge in You from Hell and from that which brings one closer to it, in word and deed. And I ask You to make every Decree that You decree concerning me good.

[*Sunan Ibn Majah* 3846]

Du'a for protection from bad Decree

اللَّهُمَّ إِنِّي أَعُوذُ بِكَ مِنْ جَهْدِ الْبَلَاءِ، وَدَرَكِ الشَّقَاءِ، وَسُوءِ الْقَضَاءِ، وَشَمَاتَةِ الأَعْدَاءِ

Allahumma innee a'oodhu bika min jahd il-balaa'i wa darak ish-shaqaa'i wa soo' il-qadaa'i wa shamaatat il-a'daa'i

I seek refuge in Allah from severe calamity, being overtaken by misery, harmful destiny, and the gloating of enemies.

[*Sahih al-Bukhari* 6616]

Du'a for contentment with Decree

اللَّهُمَّ إِنِّي أَسأَلُكَ الرِّضَا بَعْدَ القَضَاءِ

Allahumma innee as'aluka ar-ridaa ba'd al-qadaa

O Allah, I ask you for contentment after the Decree.

[*Sunan an-Nasa'i* 1305]

Chapter 2

Your decision is a *du'a* away

Du'a of Istikharah

اللَّهُمَّ إِنِّي أَسْتَخِيرُكَ بِعِلْمِكَ وَأَسْتَقْدِرُكَ بِقُدْرَتِكَ، وَأَسْأَلُكَ مِنْ فَضْلِكَ الْعَظِيمِ، فَإِنَّكَ تَقْدِرُ وَلاَ أَقْدِرُ وَتَعْلَمُ وَلاَ أَعْلَمُ وَأَنْتَ عَلاَّمُ الْغُيُوبِ اللَّهُمَّ إِنْ كُنْتَ تَعْلَمُ أَنَّ هَذَا الأَمْرَ خَيْرٌ لِي فِي دِينِي وَمَعَاشِي وَعَاقِبَةِ أَمْرِي فَاقْدُرْهُ لِي وَيَسِّرْهُ لِي ثُمَّ بَارِكْ لِي فِيهِ وَإِنْ كُنْتَ تَعْلَمُ أَنَّ هَذَا الأَمْرَ شَرٌّ لِي فِي دِينِي وَمَعَاشِي وَعَاقِبَةِ أَمْرِي فَاصْرِفْهُ عَنِّي وَاصْرِفْنِي عَنْهُ، وَاقْدُرْ لِي الْخَيْرَ حَيْثُ كَانَ ثُمَّ أَرْضِنِي بِهِ

Allahumma innee astakheeruka bi 'ilmika wa astaqdiruka bi qadratika wa as'aluka min fadlika al-'adheem fa innaka taqdiru wa la aqdiru wa ta'lamu wa la a'lamu wa anta 'allaam ul-ghuyoob. Allahumma in kunta ta'lamu anna haadha al-amra khayrun lee fee deenee wa ma'aashee wa 'aaqibati amree faqdurhu lee wa yassirhu lee thumma baarik lee feehi wa in kunta ta'lamu anna haadha al-amara sharrun lee fee deenee wa ma'aashee wa 'aaqibati amree fasrifhu 'annee wasrifnee 'anhu waqdur lil-khayra haythu kaana thumma ardinee bih

O Allah, I seek Your guidance (in making a choice) by virtue of Your knowledge, and I seek ability by virtue of Your power, and I ask You of Your great bounty. You have power, and I do not. You know, and I know not, and You are the Knower of the Unseen. O Allah, if You know that this matter [mention the thing to be decided] is good for me in my religion, my livelihood, my worldly affairs, and in the hereafter then decree it for me, make it easy for me, and bless it for me. And if You know that this matter is bad for me in my religion, my livelihood, my worldly affairs, and in the hereafter then turn it away from me turn me away from it, and decree for me the good wherever it may be and make me content with it.

[*Sahih al-Bukhari* 6382]

Chapter 3
Allah is a *du'a* away

Don't say "inshaAllah" in *du'a*

عَنْ أَنَسٍ ﷺ قَالَ قَالَ رَسُولُ اللَّهِ ﷺ إِذَا دَعَا أَحَدُكُمْ فَلْيَعْزِمْ فِي الدُّعَاءِ وَلاَ يَقُلِ اللَّهُمَّ إِنْ شِئْتَ فَأَعْطِنِي فَإِنَّ اللَّهَ لاَ مُسْتَكْرِهَ لَه

It is reported by Anas ﷺ that the Messenger of Allah ﷺ said, "When one of you calls upon Allah, let him be determined in the supplication and not say, 'O Allah, give me *if You will*,' for there is no one to coerce Allah."

[*Sahih al-Bukhari* 6338; *Sahih Muslim* 2678]

Chapter 4
Companionship is a *du'a* away

Du'a for companionship

اللَّهُمَّ ارْزُقْنِي جَلِيسًا صَالِحًا

Allahumma urzuqnee jaleesan saalihan

O Allah, grant me righteous company.

[*Jami' at-Tirmidhi* 413]

Du'a for *rizq*

رَبِّ إِنِّي لِمَآ أَنزَلْتَ إِلَيَّ مِنْ خَيْرٍ فَقِيرٌ

Rabbi innee lima anzalta ilayya min khayrin faqeer

My Lord! I am truly in need of whatever provision You may have in store for me.

[Qur'an, 28:24]

Du'a of the divorced and widowed

إِنَّا لِلَّهِ وَإِنَّا إِلَيْهِ رَاجِعُونَ

Inna lillahi wa inna ilayhi raji'oon

Verily, to Allah we belong, and to Him we will return.

[Qur'an, 2:156]

اللَّهُمَّ أْجُرْنِي فِي مُصِيبَتِي، وأَخْلِفْ لِي خَيْرًا مِنْهَا

Allahumma ajurnee fee museebati wa akhlif lee khayran minha

O Allah, reward me for my affliction and give me something better than it.

[*Sahih Muslim* 918]

The comprehensive *du'a* for marriage and family

رَبَّنَا هَبْ لَنَا مِنْ أَزْوَاجِنَا وَذُرِّيَّاتِنَا قُرَّةَ أَعْيُنٍ وَاجْعَلْنَا لِلْمُتَّقِينَ إِمَامًا

Rabbana hab lana min azwaajinaa wa dhurriyaatinaa qurrata a'yunin waj'alnaa lil-muttaqeena imaama

Our Lord, grant us delight in our spouses and our children, and make us a good example for the righteous.

[Qur'an, 25:74]

Chapter 5

Long life is a *du'a* away

Du'a for a fulfilling life

اللَّهُمَّ إِنِّي أَسْأَلُكَ فِعْلَ الْخَيْرَاتِ وَتَرْكَ الْمُنْكَرَاتِ وَحُبَّ الْمَسَاكِينِ وَإِذَا أَرَدْتَ فِي النَّاسِ فِتْنَةً فَاقْبِضْنِي إِلَيْكَ غَيْرَ مَفْتُونٍ

Allahumma innee as'aluka fi'l al-khayraat wa tark al-munkaraat wa hubb al-masaakeen wa idha aradta fi an-naasi fitnatan faqbidnee ilayka ghayra maftoon

O Allah! Indeed I ask You for righteous deeds, and avoiding evil deeds, and loving the poor. And if you have willed a trial for people, then take me to You, without being put to trial.

[*Jami' at-Tirmidhi* 3233]

Du'a for the best time of death

اللَّهُمَّ أَحْيِنِي مَا كَانَتِ الْحَيَاةُ خَيْرًا لِي وَتَوَفَّنِي إِذَا كَانَتِ الْوَفَاةُ خَيْرًا لِي

Allahumma ahyinee maa kaanat il-hayaatu khayran lee wa tawaffanee idha kaanat il-wafaatu khayran lee

O Allah, keep me alive as long as You know that life is better for me, and cause me to die when death is better for me.

[*Sahih al-Bukhari* 5671]

Chapter 6

Protection is a *du'a* away

Du'a for protection from every single harm

x3 in the morning
x3 in the evening

بِسْمِ اللَّهِ الَّذِي لاَ يَضُرُّ مَعَ اسْمِهِ شَيْءٌ فِي الأَرْضِ وَلاَ فِي السَّمَاءِ وَهُوَ السَّمِيعُ الْعَلِيمُ

Bismillahi alladhee la yadurru ma'a ismihi shay'un fee al-ardi wa la fee as-samaa'i wa huwa as-samee'u al-'aleem

In the Name of Allah, with Whose Name nothing is harmed on the earth nor in heaven, and He is the All-Hearing, the All-Knowing.

[*Jami' at-Tirmidhi* 3388]

Du'a for health and protection from trials

x3 in the morning
x3 in the evening

اللَّهُمَّ عَافِنِي فِي بَدَنِي، اللَّهُمَّ عَافِنِي فِي سَمْعِي، اللَّهُمَّ عَافِنِي فِي بَصَرِي، لاَ إِلَهَ إِلاَّ أَنْتَ، اللَّهُمَّ إِنِّي أَعُوذُ بِكَ مِنَ الْكُفْرِ وَالْفَقْرِ، اللَّهُمَّ إِنِّي أَعُوذُ بِكَ مِنْ عَذَابِ الْقَبْرِ، لاَ إِلَهَ إِلاَّ أَنْتَ

Allahumma 'aafinee fee badanee, Allahumma 'aafinee fee sam'ee, Allahumma 'aafinee fee basaree la ilaha illa anta. Allahumma innee a'oodhu bika min al-kufri wal-faqri, Allahumma innee a'oodhu bika min 'adhaab il-qabri la ilaha illa anta.

O Allah, make me healthy in my body. O Allah, make me healthy in my hearing. O Allah, make me healthy in my sight. There is no god but You. O Allah, I seek refuge with You from disbelief and poverty. O Allah, I seek refuge with You from the punishment of the grave. There is no god but You.

[*Sunan Abi Dawud* 5090]

Du'a for relief from hardship

لاَ إِلَهَ إِلاَّ أَنْتَ سُبْحَانَكَ إِنِّي كُنْتُ مِنَ الظَّالِمِينَ

La ilaha illa anta subhaanaka innee kuntu min adh-dhalimeen

There is no god but You, glorified are You, indeed I am one of the wrongdoers.

[Qur'an, 21:87]

Chapter 7

Relief is a *du'a* away

Du'a to replace anxiety with peace

اللَّهُمَّ إِنِّي عَبْدُكَ ابْنُ عَبْدِكَ ابْنُ أَمَتِكَ نَاصِيَتِي بِيَدِكَ مَاضٍ فِيَّ حُكْمُكَ عَدْلٌ فِيَّ قَضَاؤكَ أَسْأَلُكَ بِكُلِّ اسْمٍ هُوَ لَكَ سَمَّيْتَ بِهِ نَفْسَكَ أَوْ أَنْزَلْتَهُ فِي كِتَابِكَ أَوْ عَلَّمْتَهُ أَحَداً مِنْ خَلْقِكَ أَوِ اسْتَأْثَرْتَ بِهِ فِي عِلْمِ الغَيْبِ عِنْدَكَ أَنْ تَجْعَلَ القُرْآنَ رَبِيعَ قَلْبِي وَنورَ صَدْرِي وَجَلاَءَ حُزْنِي وذَهَابَ هَمِّي

Allahumma innee 'abduka ibnu 'abdika ibnu amatika naasiyatee biyadika maadin fiyya hukmuka 'adlun fiyya qadaa'uka as'aluka bi kulli ismin huwa laka sammayta bihi nafsaka aw anzaltahu fee kitaabika aw 'allamtahu ahadan min khalqika aw ista'tharta bihi fee 'ilm al-ghaybi 'indaka an taj'ala al-Qur'ana rabee'a qalbee wa noora sadree wa jalaa'a huznee wa dhahaaba hammee

O Allah, I am Your slave, and the son of Your male slave, and the son of Your female slave. My forehead is in Your Hand [i.e., You have control over me]. Your Judgement upon me is assured, and Your Decree concerning me is just. I ask You by every Name with which You have named Yourself, whether you revealed in Your Scripture, taught any one of Your creation, or kept unto Yourself in the knowledge of the Unseen that is with You, to make the Qur'an the spring of my heart, and the light of my chest, the lifting of my sadness, and the departure of my anxiety.

[*Musnad Ahmad* 1:391]

Du'a for relief from worries and debt

اللَّهُمَّ إِنِّي أَعُوذُ بِكَ مِنَ الْهَمِّ وَالْحَزَنِ، وَأَعُوذُ بِكَ مِنَ الْعَجْزِ وَالْكَسَلِ، وَأَعُوذُ بِكَ مِنَ الْجُبْنِ وَالْبُخْلِ، وَأَعُوذُ بِكَ مِنْ غَلَبَةِ الدَّيْنِ، وَقَهْرِ الرِّجَالِ

Allahumma innee a'oodhu bika min al-hammi wal-hazani wa a'oodhu bika min al-'ajzi wal-kasali wa a'oodhu bika min al-jubni wal-bukhli wa a'oodhu bika min ghalabat id-dayni wa qahr ir-rijaal

O Allah! I seek refuge in You from worry and grief, and I seek refuge in You from incapacity and laziness, and I seek refuge in You from cowardice and miserliness, and I seek refuge in You from the burden of debt and oppression of men.

[*Sahih al-Bukhari* 6369]

Du'a to remove anger

اللَّهُمَّ رَبَّ مُحَمَّدٍ اغْفِرْ لِي ذَنْبِي، وَأَذْهِبْ غَيْظَ قَلْبِي ، وَأَعِذْنِي مِنْ مُضِلَّاتِ الْفِتَنِ

Allahumma rabba Muhammadin ighfir lee dhanbee wa adhhib ghaydha qalbee wa a'idhnee min mudillaat il-fitan

O Allah, Lord of Muhammad! Forgive my sins, remove the anger of my heart, and protect me from misleading trials.

[*Musnad Ahmad* 26576]

Chapter 8

Changing your heart is a *du'a* away

Du'a to protect the heart

رَبَّنَا لَا تُزِغْ قُلُوبَنَا بَعْدَ إِذْ هَدَيْتَنَا وَهَبْ لَنَا مِن لَّدُنكَ رَحْمَةً إِنَّكَ أَنتَ ٱلْوَهَّابُ

Rabbana la tuzigh quloobanaa ba'da idh hadaytanaa wa hab lana min ludnka rahmatan innaka anta al-wahhaab

Our Lord! Do not let our hearts deviate after You have guided us, and grant us from Yourself mercy. Indeed You, You are the Bestower.

[Qur'an, 3:8]

Du'a to remove grudges

رَبَّنَا اغْفِرْ لَنَا وَلِإِخْوَانِنَا الَّذِينَ سَبَقُونَا بِالْإِيمَانِ وَلَا تَجْعَلْ فِي قُلُوبِنَا غِلًّا لِّلَّذِينَ آمَنُوا رَبَّنَا إِنَّكَ رَؤُوفٌ رَّحِيمٌ

Rabbana ighfir lana wa li-ikhwaaninaa alladheena sabaqoona bil-eemaani wa la taj'al fee quloobinaa ghillan lilladheena aamanoo rabbana innaka ra'oofun raheem

Our Lord, forgive us and our brethren who preceded us in faith, and leave no malice in our hearts towards those who believe. Our Lord, You are Clement and Merciful.

[Qur'an, 59:10]

The most frequent *du'a* of the Prophet ﷺ

يَا مُقَلِّبَ الْقُلُوبِ ثَبِّتْ قَلْبِي عَلَى دِينِكَ

Ya muqallib al-quloob thabbit qalbee 'ala deenik

O Turner of hearts, make my heart firm on Your path.

[*Jami' at-Tirmidhi* 3522]

Du'a for a heart obedient to Allah

اللَّهُمَّ مُصَرِّفَ الْقُلُوبِ
صَرِّفْ قُلُوبَنَا عَلَى طَاعَتِكَ

Allahumma musarrif al-quloob sarrif quloobanaa 'ala taa'atik

O Allah, Turner of hearts, turn our hearts towards your obedience.

[Sahih Muslim 2655]

Chapter 9

Salvation on Arafah is a *du'a* away

Du'a to be freed from the Fire

اللَّهُمَّ أَعْتِقْ رَقَبَتِي مِنَ النَّارِ،
وَأَوْسِعْ لِي مِنَ الرِّزْقِ الْحَلَالِ،
وَاصْرِفْ عَنِّي فَسَقَةَ الْجِنِّ وَالْإِنْسِ

Allahumma a'tiq raqabatee min an-naari wa-awsi' lee min ar-rizq il-halaal wasrif 'annee fasaqat al-jinni wal-ins

O Allah, free my neck from the Fire, bestow on me halal sustenance, and avert from me corrupt jinn and men.

[Ibn Abi Dunya]

The best *du'a* on the day of Arafah

لَا إِلَهَ إِلَّا اللَّهُ وَحْدَهُ لَا شَرِيكَ لَهُ
لَهُ الْمُلْكُ وَلَهُ الْحَمْدُ وَهُوَ عَلَى كُلِّ شَيْءٍ قَدِير

La ilaha illa Allahu wahdahu la shareeka lahu lahul-mulku wa lahul-hamdu wa huwa 'ala kulli shay'in qadeer

There is no true deity but God alone who has no partner; to Him belongs the dominion, to Him praise is due, and He is able to do all things.

[Sunan at-Tirmidhi 3585]

Chapter 10

The best of everything is a *du'a* away

Du'a that covers all needs

اللَّهُمَّ إِنِّي أَسْأَلُكَ الْعَافِيَةَ فِي الدُّنْيَا وَالآخِرَةِ

Allahumma innee as'aluka al-'afiyah fid-dunyaa wal-aakhirah

O Allah, I ask you for *'afiyah* in this life and the next.

[Sunan Ibn Majah 3871]

Du'a for the best of both worlds

اللَّهُمَّ اغْفِرْ لَنَا، وَارْحَمْنَا، وَآتِنَا
فِي الدُّنْيَا حَسَنَةً، وَفِي الْآخِرَةِ
حَسَنَةً، وَقِنَا عَذَابَ النَّارِ

Allahumma ighfir lana warhamnaa wa 'aatinaa fid-dunyaa hasanatan wa fil-aakhirati hasanatan wa qinaa 'adhaab an-naar

O Allah, forgive us, have mercy on us, and grant us the best of this life, and the best of the afterlife, and protect us from the fire.

[Al-Adab al-Mufrad 633]

A comprehensive *du'a* to recite in salah

اللَّهُمَّ اغْفِرْ لِي، وَارْحَمْنِي، وَاهْدِنِي، وَارْزُقْنِي

Allahumma ighfir lee warhamnee wahdinee warzuqnee

O Allah, forgive me, show mercy to me, guide me, and provide for me.

[Sahih Muslim 2697]

Reflections

Reflections